THE
LANDSCAPES
OF
SOMERSET

DAVID SELLMAN & ROGER EVANS

COUNTRYSIDE BOOKS
NEWBURY, BERKSHIRE

COUNTRYSIDE BOOKS
3 Catherine Road
Newbury, Berkshire

To view our complete range of books,
please visit us at
www.countrysidebooks.co.uk

ISBN 1 85306 807 1

Designed by Peter Davies, Nautilus Design
Produced through MRM Associates Ltd., Reading
Typeset by Techniset Typesetters, Newton-le-Willows
Printed in Italy

CONTENTS

INTRODUCTION

'Mongst the hills o' Somerset
Wisht I was a-roamin yet!

JAMES WHITCOMB RILEY, *Amongst the Hills o' Somerset*

Somerset is the land of the summer people. It is blessed with a wonderful variety of landscape, from heather-covered high moorland to the rich farmland of the valleys; from dramatic steep-sided cliffs and gorges to miles and miles of sand dunes and golden beaches. The county is a largely agricultural one and over the centuries, even Somerset's wilder regions such as Exmoor have been tamed by man's creativity.

Long ago, much of Somerset was beneath the sea. The areas we now know as Sedgemoor, or the Somerset Levels and the Moors, were almost constantly flooded. For thousands of years, the plant life which could survive in such areas thrived and has left behind deep layers of peat between the Polden Ridge and the Mendip Hills.

Welcome to Somerset.

On the other side of the Poldens, where the sea reached far inland, layer upon layer of silt was deposited to create the heavy clay of the Sedgemoor area that, for so many years, provided the raw material for a thriving brick and tile industry. Wrapped around these watery lowlands are the famous hills of the Blackdowns, the Quantocks, the Brendons and, of course, the Mendips.

Set in this rich landscape are historic towns and peaceful villages that continue to delight residents and visitors alike. With the help of David Sellman's superb photographs, I would like to take you on a tour of the county which I am proud to call my home.

Roger Evans

DOONE COUNTRY

To me they seem Spartan and untiring, these women on the out-lying hill farms. Farm labour is scarce so that at sheep-shearing and threshing the farmers co-operate, and the wife has a dozen to cook for while carrying on her usual routine ...

BERTA LAWRENCE *A Somerset Journal* (1951)

The visitor to Malmesmead, in the valley of the East Lyn river, is faced with a choice of ways to cross the river known as Badgworthy Water (pronounced *badgery*). The old packhorse bridge stands as testament to the age of this hamlet, and alongside the bridge is the river ford for the more adventurous. Those crossing the river here will be making the journey from Somerset into Devon, the county boundary running along the centre of the stream. Overlooking the scene is Lorna Doone Farm, a reminder, if one is needed, that it was the wild and remote valleys and moorland above Malmesmead that R. D. Blackmore was to choose as the setting for his famous novel *Lorna Doone*.

Further downstream, Badgworthy Water is joined by Oare Water as it cascades down from Robbers Bridge, and these in turn run into the East Lyn River. It is Badgworthy Valley which is now popularly known as the Doone Valley. This valley, apart from its literary connections, is well worth exploring. It boasts a wonderfully atmospheric landscape with rock strewn streams

It was here, according to legend, that the Doones settled in Hoccombe Combe after being exiled from Scotland in the 17th century. They became outlaws and robbed and terrorised the local Exmoor families, carrying off the young Lorna when she was still just a child. Her fate was to be a forced marriage to Carver Doone. However, she was rescued by John Ridd, who had discovered a way into the hidden valley. There he was to meet Lorna and secretly woo her and eventually rescue her from the Doones. The conclusion of the story takes place at Oare church (*inset*), famous as the place where Carver Doone shot Lorna.

WHERE CELTS AND SAXONS FARMED

Exmoor, where they have nine months winter and three months hard labour.

A TRADITIONAL EXMOOR SAYING

Whilst large parts of Exmoor have a natural, wild and often bleak appearance, as though untouched by human hand, the whole landscape has been very much shaped by mankind. In Mesolithic times, the inhabitants hunted and fished, cut trees, cultivated in a small way and grazed what animals they could. Slowly the landscape changed. Later came the Celts and then the Saxons, who built their own farms and villages and established the settlement pattern which can still be found today.

Gradually the trees were cleared, leaving the uplands with their poorer soil to the wild deer and ponies, whilst the richer lower lands were cultivated to create suitable grazing for sheep and cattle. In 1818 the Crown sold Exmoor to John Knight, who commenced intensive farming and changed the face of Exmoor forever. Today the moor is a national park of over 170,000 acres of deep-sided tree-covered combes, heather covered rolling moors and fast flowing rivers, which run down to the craggy and often spectacular coastline.

The village of Withypool, with its scattering of cottages along the River Barle, lies in the heart of Exmoor, where it survives largely unspoilt thanks to the lack of access for tourist coaches. South of the village is Withypool Hill with its Bronze Age stone circle of 37 low stones, all that remains of the original 100 or so.

Nearby Tarr Steps (*inset*) is a set of large flat stones which form a 170 ft clapper bridge crossing the River Barle. It is almost certainly medieval, built for use by packhorse traders. It is one of the oldest clapper bridges in England. No form of bonding is used to keep the stones in place, simply their massive weight where they can rest on piers which project either side of the flat stones. The weight of the stones proved sufficient to keep them in place for hundreds of years, although in recent times severe weather conditions with flash floods have occasionally caused them to shift.

An Ancient Port Where Poets Waxed Lyrical

I am hungry to be interrupted
Forever and ever amen
O Person from Porlock come quickly
And bring my thoughts to an end.

Stevie Smith, *Thoughts about the Person from Porlock*

The sea used to reach all the way into Porlock and the town's prosperity once partly depended on fishing and seaborne trade. As the sea retreated it left Porlock high and dry a mile inland, and so Porlock Weir was created out of necessity. The small harbour was built in 1422 and the spot was called Weir, reflecting the rows of stakes which were driven into the shoreline in order to trap salmon. Porlock Weir shelters under Worthy Wood and has a pebbled beach and a petrified forest, which dates back to 4000 BC.

The cottage called Oyster Perch hints at the one-time famous oyster beds, which rivalled those of Colchester. These beds were a well kept local secret, whose

shelters beneath the dominating Bossington Hill, with its steep wooded slopes where the rare evergreen oak can be found. The colour-washed thatched cottages with rounded chimneys and cottage gardens sit amidst magnificent walnut trees, beneath whose shade the fast flowing stream rushes by on its way to cross the pebbled beach at nearby Porlock Bay. Several cottages offer cream teas for the many walkers who frequent this beautiful corner of Somerset, a favourite spot for many an artist.

Here can be found excellent walking country with routes to Hurlestone Point, with its magnificent views across

location was marked by the presence of the whitewashed cottages. The thatched Ship Inn dates back to the 16th century and the neighbouring Anchor Hotel to the 19th century. Behind here were lime kilns which once produced fertiliser.

The tiny hamlet of Bossington (*inset*) owned by the National Trust,

Porlock Bay, and Selworthy Beacon, perhaps the most scenic part of the whole Exmoor National Park. Both feature on the long distance path, the South West Way, and from their heights can be seen South Wales across the channel and exceptional views over Exmoor.

THE WILDS OF EXMOOR

And often when no cause appears
The mountain-ponies prick their ears.

WILLIAM WORDSWORTH, *The Danish Boy – A Fragment*

Between Porlock and Lynton, Exmoor rises rapidly and dramatically from the North Somerset coast to heights in excess of 1,000 ft within just a few miles. From such heights, numerous streams descend the deep sided and densely wooded valleys. Robbers Bridge (*inset*) crosses one such stream, Weir Water, before it cascades its way down

through Oare, where it becomes Oare Water, and then onto Malmesmead and the East Lyn River. Robbers Bridge itself is unexceptional other than that it is set in some of the most beautiful scenery in the west of England, scenery often unappreciated by the motorist negotiating his way along the narrow winding lanes, especially in the summer as cars jostle for position.

This part of the Exmoor Forest is best appreciated by the walker and near to Robbers Bridge can be found a car park. The heavily wooded hillsides offer wonderful shade for families to picnic, away from the excesses of the summer sun. The bridge is believed to take its name from the villainous Doone family, who frequented this area in Blackmore's novel, *Lorna Doone*.

Across the moor, the wild red deer and Exmoor ponies roam free. The short and stocky Exmoor pony is possibly the hardiest breed in our islands, toughened by the harsh wind-blown rains and snow which are a regular winter feature of these exposed uplands. The Exmoor Pony Society was formed in 1921 to ensure the survival of this rare breed, which is closer to the true native wild horse than any other breed of pony. Not all ponies on the moor are true bred Exmoor ponies, but those that are typically have an oatmeal coloured flattened muzzle, shorter than average ears and a coat whose dark brown colour matures to dark honey as the years progress.

The red deer are the largest of our native species and, whilst present in much greater numbers than the ponies, are much more difficult to spot. Their days are spent in the dense woodland areas or lying up in the deep bracken. At night they graze freely on the open moor, and so dawn and dusk are perhaps the best times to see them before they merge once more into the background.

PACKHORSE COUNTRY AT ALLERFORD

... and here at this little place where boates unlade the coale, the packhorse comes, and takes it in sacks and so carryes it to the place all about ...

CELIA FIENNES, *Through England on a Sidesaddle*

Allerford is a delightful little hamlet set just off the main road between Minehead and Porlock. It nestles quietly beneath steep sided, heavily wooded hills which shelter it from the sea and south-westerly winds. The scattered houses lie never far from the stream which flows from Tivington Common and Luccombe Hill and passes beneath the hamlet's two-arched packhorse bridge (*inset*) on its way to Porlock Bay.

For centuries packhorses were the only practical means of transport in this hill country, and several such bridges survive in the area with further fine examples at Horner and Dunster. But Allerford's, though not the oldest, is perhaps the best. The parapets of the cobbled bridge are deliberately low to permit the passing of wide loads carried on the backs of pack animals. As is usual with such bridges, there is a ford alongside as an alternative crossing in drier conditions and for horse-drawn vehicles.

Within the village is the Allerford Rural Life Museum, which contains implements and crafts from bygone days in West Somerset. A particular delight is the Victorian schoolroom, complete with wooden desks, ink wells and chalk writing boards. There are even children's clothes for dressing up and re-capturing the spirit of the rural life of yesteryear.

This is ideal walking country, with paths to nearby Selworthy village, Selworthy Beacon and Bossington Hill, or through Bossington village to Porlock Bay and on to the harbour at Porlock Weir.

Just across the A39 is Piles Mill, a small and quite complete cornmill with its 10 ft overshot wheel. Here, where the main road crosses the stream, can be found a beehive-shaped stone structure, if it's not too overgrown to be seen. Its reputed use was as an ash house to store the ash from the baking ovens. In spring the ash would be spread on the allotments or kitchen gardens. More recent opinion is that it served as a dipping well, the spring water having been filtered through the gravel floor. The local ladies would visit with their buckets and scoops to dip into the clear waters. Local theories that this once served as a pixie house should not be taken seriously by the visitor!

MINEHEAD, THE SAFEST HARBOUR

Our road lay through woods rising perpendicularly from the sea.

DOROTHY WORDSWORTH

The harbour at Minehead and the delightful row of cottages along its approach reflect the origins of Minehead as a small fishing community which once became a sea trading port. Daniel Defoe described it as the best port and safest harbour along the south coast of the Bristol Channel. The present quay was built around 1610 by George Luttrell at a cost of £5,000 and was extended in 1682. With the building of the harbour, Minehead developed from a fishing port to a sea trading centre. Grain, bark and cloth were exported, with wool, destined for Taunton's serge makers, and hides coming in from Ireland. By 1701 the town boasted 30 ships manned by 137 seamen.

Beyond the harbour, a path takes you through level parkland to a steep path which leads up onto the open moorland of North Hill, with its outstanding views of Exmoor and the sea. It is from here, along the sea front, that the long distance coastal footpath commences.

Above the harbour, Higher Town sits on the steep-sided hill, its narrow, cottage-lined streets leading to the 15th-century stone-built church of St Michael, which has a wagon roof in the Devon style with no division between nave and chancel. On many a stormy night, the church served as a landmark for local fishermen.

The nature of Minehead began to change in the early 19th century when, with improvements to the roads and the arrival of the railway, tourism was to develop and become the town's saviour.

Now, the two miles of pebbles and sand dominated by North Hill, which offers some shelter from the south-westerly winds, are amongst the main attractions, and draw holidaymakers year after year.

Tourism has also been the saviour of the West Somerset Railway which, closed by Beeching in 1971, re-opened under private ownership in 1976, providing visitors with the opportunity to see the old steam trains still in active service.

PICTURE POSTCARD PERFECTION AT SELWORTHY

The cottage homes of England! By thousands on her plains,
They are smiling o'er the silvery brooks, and round the hamlet-fanes.

FELICIA HEMANS, *The Homes of England*

Selworthy is arguably the prettiest village in England. Separated from fine coastal views by the towering Selworthy Beacon and Bossington Hill rising to over 1,000 ft, Selworthy is obliged to face Exmoor rather than the sea.

Owned by the National Trust, the hamlet has seven lattice-windowed, thatched cottages with tall rounded chimneys. The cottages, which look much older than they really are, were built in 1828 for Sir Thomas Dyke Acland as housing for his estate workers.

And what an idyllic spot this is, with the cottages clustered around the village green beneath the steep, wooded hill, and magnificent ancient walnut trees to complete the scene and delight the visitor's eye.

Overlooking the small group of cottages, Selworthy's white-painted, 15th-century church (*inset*) is well worth a visit. Its famous, coloured wagon roof is ornamented with angels, shields and fine bosses. The remains of a medieval cross can be found in the churchyard, albeit the head is missing. From here there are clear views across to Dunkery Beacon. Also not to be missed are the 14th-century stone tithe barn and dovecote.

Next to the church is a car park, from where a path leads to Bury Castle, an Iron Age settlement. This was an ancient enclosure, some 200 ft in diameter, where the outline of the outer defences which formed the stock pens can still be seen. Nearby on Selworthy Beacon are several round barrows, although they are indistinct today.

As small and quaint as this village appears, it has a long history and one which belies the tranquillity the present setting suggests. For this was once the home of Eadgyth of Selworthy, Edith the Fair. She was the sister of Harold Godwyn, the Harold who, thanks to a Norman archer at the Battle of Hastings, lost the battle when William the Conqueror invaded. Harold was lord of the manor of Dulverton and, with his sister Edith, waged a war of vengeance against Ælfgar of Porlock, son of Leofric. Ælfgar held the power in much of West Somerset and was a popular leader, far more so than his neighbour Harold. So Harold and his Selworthy sister joined forces and invaded Porlock in 1052. It doesn't seem possible that such a peaceful spot could have harboured such a vengeful lady.

ENCHANTED CASTLE AND SPINNING YARNS

The stately homes of England, How beautiuful they stand!
Amidst their tall ancestral trees, O'er all the pleasant land.

FELICIA HEMANS, *The Homes of England*

With lofty hill after lofty hill, separated by deeply cleft wooded valleys, the Dunster landscape has a distinctly alpine feel. The old town itself nestles in the Avill Valley, between Vinegar Hill on one side and Grabbist Hill on the other.

At the seaward end of Grabbist Hill stands the Conygar Tower. An 18th-century folly, it reaches up through the trees to provide a pleasing addition to the view from nearby fairytale Dunster Castle standing across the valley.

This is an exceptionally well preserved medieval settlement, with cobbled roads, a castle and a 17th-century octagonal yarn market. If there is any place in Somerset more inclined to inspire ghost stories and legends and exclamations of 'Here be dragons!', I have yet to find it. Indeed it was here, according to legend, that King Arthur met St Carranog, who, at Arthur's request, tamed the local dragon which had terrorised the neighbouring villages of Carhampton and Cleeve.

Dunster Castle is amongst the oldest continuously inhabited castles in the country. It was a Saxon towered fortress, owned by Aluric and built on a natural mound. It was taken by the Normans in the 11th century and in 1376 it was bought by Elizabeth Luttrell of Quantoxhead for 5,000 marks. Thereafter it remained in the possession of the Luttrell family until 1976, when Lt Colonel Walter Luttrell gave it to the National Trust.

Legends and traditions live on in Dunster. The Luttrell Arms, a former residence of the abbots of Cleeve, is a well maintained hotel with several medieval features. Here the local custom of burning the ashen faggot is still practised on Christmas Eve, a reminder of how the shepherds helped to keep the young Jesus warm. And on May Day a relic of the hobby horse tradition survives with the "sailors' 'oss" processing from the castle down through the village, accompanied by its crew of morris men revellers.

COASTAL SPLENDOUR

The ship was cheered, the harbour cleared,
Merrily did we drop
Below the kirk, below the hill,
Below the light-house top.

SAMUEL TAYLOR COLERIDGE, *Rime of the Ancient Mariner*

The small seaside resort of Blue Anchor, with its long open beach, is most noteworthy for its strange geological formations: tall cliffs of red sandstone closely followed by cliffs striped with white alabaster. This material was widely used for carving memorials, particularly in the medieval period, and many examples can be found across the county. Nowadays, Blue Anchor is populated by numerous caravan sites, and the West Somerset Railway has one of its stations here, where well maintained steam engines provide access to Minehead and Bishops Lydeard.

As quiet as Blue Anchor bay may appear today (*opposite*), it was a different story just a week before Christmas in 1941. Two objects had been spotted floating in the bay, about half a mile offshore and about the same distance apart. They looked like parts of aircraft wings, belonging perhaps to a German aircraft which had ditched in nearby St Audries' Bay the month before. Two local fishermen went out in their small boat to investigate as the tide rapidly retreated. Approaching the first object, they reached out with a boathook to haul themselves closer. It was a fatal mistake, for the object turned out to be a parachute mine. There was a massive explosion, and all that was left was a huge crater being lapped by the waves.

The nearby harbour town of Watchet (*inset*), with its pebble beach, was a busy port in the 19th century when the mineral railway brought raw materials down from the Brendon Hills, taking them on to South Wales and bringing back coal on the return.

Above the harbour stands a hill on which can be found the 15th-century church of St Decuman. These are the church, hill and harbour to which Samuel Taylor Coleridge refers in his *Rime of the Ancient Mariner*. The harbour in recent times has been converted into a marina, where boats and small ships can find safe mooring. Watchet possesses a wonderful town museum, full of fascinating memorabilia reflecting the old days of the town. A ship museum has also opened in recent years, where locally built craft can be studied.

THE ROMANCE OF STEAM

Since railways came into existence, the necessity of not missing the train has taught us to take account of minutes whereas among the Romans ... the notion not of minutes but even of fixed hours barely existed.

MARCEL PROUST, *Remembrance of Things Past*

The 20-mile stretch of the West Somerset Railway, the longest privately owned railway in the country, recaptures the nostalgic age of steam. Climb aboard one of the old-fashioned carriages, and sit back and enjoy the scenery, as the journey takes you from Bishops Lydeard station alongside the Quantock Hills and down to the sea. If the weather is fine, the trip can even be extended along the coast of Somerset and North Devon on the paddle steamer *Waverley*. No fewer than ten restored stations can be admired, along with signal boxes and engine sheds. Each station has its own character and charm, as befits a railway of yesteryear.

The West Somerset Railway Company was incorporated in 1857 by an Act of Parliament. The company was authorised to raise £120,000 to open the first section of the railway. It was in 1864 that the branch line from Taunton to Watchet was completed and in 1874 it was further extended all the way down to Minehead. Originally a broad gauge line, it was converted to the standard gauge in 1882. Dr Beeching's ruthless axe fell on the line in 1971, and there then began a brief period of decay. Fortunately a private company was formed which re-opened the line from Bishops Lydeard to Minehead. The link to Taunton is completed with the local bus service. Both steam and diesel trains operate along the line and, whilst the heaviest activity is during the tourist season, trains run throughout the year including the Santa specials at Christmas time.

There was a time when two lines were operated between Minehead and Dunster, such was the volume of traffic – but not so these days.

OF CLIFFS AND SMUGGLERS

*No, my friends emerge
beneath the wide wide heaven – and view again
the man-steepled tract magnificent
of hilly fields and meadows, and the sea.*

SAMUEL TAYLOR COLERIDGE, *This Lime Tree Bower My Prison*

The village of Kilve lies astride the A39 in one direction and in the other Kilve's Pill. This is a brook which runs from Holford down into Kilve, past the ruined chantry and on to the beach, described by Wordsworth as Kilve's 'delightful shore', where it joins what Southey described as Kilve's 'green sea'. Whilst the poets waxed lyrical about the shore, they would have been less inspired by the disused oil retort which now tries to hide behind the invading wall of ivy (*inset*). This brick and cast-iron retort is all that survives of a failed attempt in the 1920s by the Shaline Company to turn Kilve into the oil producing centre of the south-west. In 1916 it was discovered that the cliffs contained bituminous liassic shale, potentially capable of yielding oil. Trials proved the venture to be too costly to justify the low yield achievable, and the retort survives as a relic.

Closer to the village, the ruins of Kilve Priory also remind us of times gone by. It was founded in 1329 by Simon de Furneaux and used in the 19th century as a storage depot for smugglers bringing in brandy under the noses of the customs men. In 1848, when the customs men got too close for comfort and it was realised that a raid on their secret store was imminent, the smugglers set fire to the brandy, which blew up, leaving the priory building as we see it today.

The cliffs along the shoreline here are rich in ammonite fossils and the beach is striated with layers of shale, which form rock pools aplenty. Beneath the rocks, at low tide, can be found conger eels, which used to be hunted, until recent times, with dogs and spears, in a practice referred to as *glatting*.

QUANTOCK'S SYLVAN COMBES

Upon smooth Quantock's airy ridge we moved
Unchecked or loitered 'mid her sylvan combes.

WILLIAM WORDSWORTH

The Quantock Hills rise from sea level to over 900 ft in just a couple of miles and offer spectacular views across the Bristol Channel to the coast of South Wales and the Black Mountains beyond, and inland to the Mendip Hills, the Blackdowns and the wilderness of

Exmoor. This is wonderful walking country, with a ridge path that runs from one end of the hills to the other, from above Bagborough to Quantoxhead. The many peaks along the way include Cothlestone Beacon, Wills Neck, Danesborough, Lydeard Hill, Thorncombe and Beacon Hill. Running down from the ridge on either side of these hills are deep cut combes, which provide shelter for the large numbers of wild red deer.

Seven Wells Combe and Cockercombe are deep and leafy. Holford glen is magical, and a wonderful walk can be found from the village green car park at Holford, up through Hodders, Somerton and Stert Combes to Halsway Post, across to Bicknoller Post, and then back through Shepherd's Combe, Lady's Edge and Hodders Combe for a home-cooked meal at the idyllically set Stella's Tea Gardens. It's a satisfying way to end a 6-mile walk in what I consider to be the finest walking in the country.

The Quantock villages are few in number and remain unspoilt by development, protected perhaps by their position in this Area of Outstanding Natural Beauty. Crowcombe is one such village (*inset*), which has altered little in 400 years. It can boast a 14th-century market cross and a church house dating back to 1515, within which the churchwardens brewed ales to raise funds. The building survives remarkably well, with many interesting architectural features.

The church has a 14th-century red sandstone tower and an exceptional fan-vaulted ceiling. The bench ends are adorned with wonderful carvings which include a mermaid, a green man and a small naked man battling with dragons. This is hunting country, and the walls of the Carew Arms, Crowcombe's village inn, are adorned with stags' horns and pictures of hunting parties.

MONUMENTAL RECOGNITION ON BLACKDOWN'S HILLS

Bury the Great Duke
With an empire's lamentation;
Let us bury the Great Duke
To the noise of the mourning of a mighty nation;

ALFRED LORD TENNYSON, *Ode on the death of the Duke of Wellington*

The Blackdown Hills, another of Somerset's Areas of Outstanding Natural Beauty, are perhaps the least well known of Somerset's uplands. They lie on the Somerset-Devon border, extending on the northern side as far as Wellington, where the steep and wooded scarp faces the town and the M5 motorway. Commanding the head of the scarp is the Wellington monument. At 175 ft high, it is visible for many miles around and is a familiar landmark for the summer tourist travelling down the motorway. At night the monument glows in the darkness, floodlit by spotlights around the base.

It was constructed in 1817 to commemorate the Duke of Wellington's victory over Napoleon at Waterloo. The Duke, whose real name was Wellesley, took the name for his dukedom from the town, although he had no actual connections with the area. The column was originally intended to support a huge cast iron statue of the Duke – but the money ran out. The column, shorter than intended, was completed after the Duke's death in 1852. A spiral stairway winds up through the centre of the column, but in recent years the entrance has been sealed following an incident involving an uninvited cow.

Beyond the monument, the Blackdowns form an open wind-swept plateau, which sweeps gently down to Cullompton and Chard. There are no towns in this unspoilt part of the county, just villages and farmsteads which have maintained their natural rural charm. They find shelter from the wind in the deep-cut valleys and are connected by a network of hedge-covered, high banked lanes which criss-cross the system of enclosed fields.

CASTLE, CRICKET AND THE CHELSEA OF THE WEST

This castle hath a pleasant seat; the air
Nimbly and sweetly recommends itself
Unto our gentle senses

WILLIAM SHAKESPEARE, *Macbeth*

Taunton, which can trace its origins back to pre-Roman times, is the county town of Somerset and is situated astride the River Tone. Landscaped riverside walks, Vivary Park public gardens and the churches of St James and St Mary enhance this major shopping centre. The Perpendicular church of St Mary Magdalene has a magnificently ornate tower, which, built in four stages, stands at 163 ft high. It is certainly the tallest in Somerset and arguably one of the finest in the land.

It was here in Saxon times that King Ine built a fortress, and in 1685 the Duke of Monmouth was proclaimed king in the town centre. Taunton Castle dates back to the 12th century and is now home to the Somerset County Museum. In the mid-17th century, it was besieged a number of times during the period of the English Civil War and defended for Parliament most vigorously by Bridgwater's Admiral Blake. After the Monmouth Rebellion, it was in the great hall of the castle that Judge Jeffreys conducted the Bloody Assizes, during which 526 cases were heard in three days; 19 of the rebels were hung, drawn and quartered in the town centre, 139 met a similar end elsewhere and the majority of the survivors were transported to the West Indies to work as slaves in the plantations.

Today the only battles are of a sporting nature, and it is in Taunton that the county cricket team, which dates back to 1875, has its home. At the county ground, there is a cricket museum with much memorabilia and reminders of the glory years of Somerset cricket when stars such as Ian Botham, Viv Richards and Joel Garner led the county to its many major successes.

In modern times Taunton has gained renown for its annual flower show, described as the 'Chelsea of the West'. In the town centre, the roads converge to form a triangular central space, where the old market cross stands. Tudor House nearby dates back to the 14th century.

SUNRISE ON THE LEVELS

Tho Venice boast, Brent is as famed a seat,
For here we live in seas, and sail thro' every street;
And this great privilege we farther gain,
We never are obliged to pray for rain.

WILLIAM DIAPER, *Brent*

Burrow Mump (*inset*) stands proud from the thousands of surrounding low-lying moors. A mere 70 ft in height and crowned with the ruins of St Michael's church, this natural hill was left as an island after the rivers had etched away the softer surrounding land.

With the encircling hills capturing the rainfall and then releasing it into the levels around Burrow Bridge, winter flooding of large areas is an annual certainty. But such flooding results in some of the lushest grazing land in the country, once the floods have receded. To the east of Burrow Mump, the huge expanse of Southlake Moor is a regular winter lake (*opposite*). Retaining walls built by the Abbots of Glastonbury to keep the waters out now serve to keep the waters in, protecting areas downstream from winter flooding.

Where the River Tone meets the River Parrett stands Burrow Bridge, which in ancient times served as a river port. Until the medieval period, this was the first bridge inland to cross the River Parrett. It was also a convenient stopping point, where craft could moor up whilst waiting to take advantage of the tides to carry them upstream to Langport or downstream to Bridgwater. Such an important crossing point needed to be defended by a hill fort on the Mump. This also protected the approach to King Alfred's headquarters nearby. The Mump eventually became the property of the National Trust; it was gifted in 1946 by Major A. G. Barrett as a memorial to those who fell in the Second World War.

Rebel Town and Home of the Carnival

Now Blake was an Admiral true as gold,
And he walk'd by the English sea;
And when he was told of the Dutchman bold,
A merry laugh laughed he,
A merry laugh laughed he.

Frederick E. Weatherly, *The Admiral's Broom*

Standing on the tidal River Parrett, Bridgwater has a long and rich history. Whilst records date back to the year 800, it was not until around 1200 that Bridgwater gained in prominence when the first bridge was built across the river. From then on the tall masted sailing ships coming up from the Bristol Channel were obliged to moor up at the town's quaysides, and from there cargoes destined for central Somerset would be transferred to barges for their onward journey. Bridgwater thereafter developed as a port and even had its own

shipbuilding industry and dock, which now survives as a marina.

In 1598 Robert Blake was born in the town; his family were importers and exporters. His exposure to the ships along the river must have whetted his appetite for the sea. It was during the Civil War that Blake, whose statue now takes pride of place in the town centre (*inset*), gained a considerable reputation as a strategist and leader, skills which he took with him when he revolutionised the English navy. In later years, Nelson was to describe him as the finest admiral the nation ever had. He triumphed over the Royalist privateers, the French navy, the Dutch and the Spanish, not to mention the Barbary pirates.

Today the town is perhaps best known for its fair and carnival, both of which come late in the year. The fair, which dates back to medieval times, now lasts four days and commences on the last Wednesday in September. It is one of the largest in the land. But it is the carnival which gives Bridgwater its worldwide fame. Developing from the Guy Fawkes celebrations after the Gunpowder Plot in 1605, this is the largest night-time carnival procession anywhere in the world. Over a hundred entries can be guaranteed, including giant 100 ft long floats illuminated with tens of thousands of light bulbs. The glow over the town on carnival night can be seen for miles. Whilst the procession also graces some of the other Somerset towns, it is at Bridgwater that it is at its largest and only in Bridgwater is there the squibbing display, in which over a hundred giant fireworks are held aloft and fired simultaneously in the town's High Street.

Where the Lonely Lighthouse Stands

... an inconsiderable parish of poor renters and cottagers, who existed without hot dinners, silk clothing, carriages of pleasure, mahogany furniture, clocks, watches, or even kettles, notwithstanding the profusion of these at present.

Richard Locke, surveyor, on Burnham in 1750.

Few seaside resorts can boast two lighthouses, but Burnham-on-Sea is one of them. Until the end of the 18th century, Burnham was no more than a fishing hamlet, where the fishermen's wives would put lanterns in their windows to guide the menfolk home. It was in 1801 that the Reverend David Davies built the first lighthouse here. By 1832 Trinity House had taken over, and the town had two lighthouses. The more recent is the High Light, a 120 ft high white, brick built tower, which stands proud over the town from its inshore position. But more unusual is the eight-legged Low Light, which stands on the beach. In the Victorian period Burnham developed as a seaside resort, with its own rail terminus and a steamer link to South Wales.

In addition to the lighthouses, the town can also boast a pier and the church of St Andrew which, having been built on sand around 1315, now leans to compete with the tower at Pisa.

From the sea front at Burnham, the beach runs several miles up past Berrow with its golf links and on to the dramatic cliffs of Brean Down. Whilst the beach is several miles long, it is also a few miles deep at low tide; the mud flats here extend for miles beyond the sand line with little drop in the level. This means that the tide goes out an extremely long way but comes in very rapidly as high tide approaches. In places the sands can be quite treacherous, and the visitor is advised to heed the warning notices.

Such a vast expanse of tidal mudflats makes Bridgwater Bay of special importance to the thousands of wading birds and wildfowl, which justifies the bay's classification as a nature reserve. Across the River Parrett from Burnham is the hamlet of Steart, where excellent gazebo hides can be used by the visitor to view the thousands of shelduck, wigeon, curlew, redshank, knot and dunlin and the scores of other species which frequent this wintering ground of international importance.

VICTORIAN WESTON-SUPER-MARE

... studded with temples of health and mansions of the rich, and its ocean bounded valley is thickly covered with handsome habitations.

FROM A BRISTOL DIRECTORY, 1859

Three miles of sandy beaches, a promenade to match and the Grand Pier are the most notable of Weston-super-Mare's landmarks. One glance along the seafront properties gives away the origins of the seaside town, much loved especially by visitors from the Midlands.

Although life began as a small fishing village, it was during the days of Queen Victoria that the village grew from its tiny population of around 100 to a seaside resort of 20,000 which since then has expanded to the 70,000 or so of today.

To the south, the town and its beach are overlooked by Brean Down with its ancient hill settlement and Napoleonic fort. To the north, Worlebury Hill, also the site of an ancient Iron Age hill fort, dominates the skyline. It was the beach and the sea water in between these hills that doctors in the 18th century extolled as health giving, although how anyone could be persuaded to drink the brown sea water of the Bristol Channel defies understanding. Conveniently positioned for the wealthy gentry of Bristol and Bath, it soon became a popular resort. In 1810 the first hotel, the Royal, opened. By 1822 the town had a hotel, two inns and a guide book for tourists. The seaside resort had arrived, and in 1841 it was large enough to justify its own station on Brunel's Bristol to Exeter railway.

During the Second World War, Weston played host to large numbers of American troops prior to the D-Day landings, the beach being used to practise their manoeuvres. Birnbeck Island was also home to a team of military boffins who were developing secret weapons.

Today it is just the tourists and the famous Weston donkeys which invade the beach. Towards the end of the summer, there is now an annual motorbike race on the beach; the sand is bulldozed to create a giant course which provides an incredible spectacle of roaring engines and flying sand. Don't stand too close!

ASHTON'S WINDMILL

Behold! A giant am I!
Aloft here in my tower,
With my granite jaws I devour
The maize, and the wheat, and the rye,
And grind them into flour.

HENRY WADSWORTH LONGFELLOW, *The Windmill*

Close to the village of Chapel Allerton can be found the Ashton windmill (*opposite and inset*), the only one in the county with all its working parts intact – the sails, the stones and the machinery. It is typical of Somerset tower mills and dates from around 1770. The cap, the upper part of the mill, which needs to turn so that the sails face into the wind, is operated by hand. When it was a working mill, some locals considered that it gave too coarse a grind for making flour, and hence the wheat for bread would be taken to the watermill at Henton. It ceased as a working mill in 1927 and then lay idle until the 1950s, when a Mr C. Clarke set about its restoration. It is now in the ownership of Sedgemoor District Council and can usually be visited on Sundays during the summer season, when a team of volunteers welcomes visitors.

Another fine example of a Somerset windmill is on the edge of the Polden Hills at Walton. Records for a windmill on that site date back to a post mill in 1342, but the present mill is much more recent and only dates back to around 1790. It stands today as a private home, with its machinery and its thatched cap long since gone. From its position high on Walton Hill, the viewer can look across the low flatlands of the Somerset Levels to High Ham on the opposite hill, with its 26 ft stone tower windmill from around 1822. This one still has its machinery and is somewhat special as the only windmill in the whole country to retain its thatched cap.

If further proof is required of the early presence of windmills in Somerset, there is in St Mary's church at Bishops Lydeard, an excellent bench-end carving dating back to about 1550, which depicts a post mill, and a similar one can be found at North Cadbury church.

THE POTTER AND POLDEN PRIDE

And as the sun drew down to west,
We climbed the toilsome Polden crest.

Thomas Hardy, *A Trampwoman's Tragedy*

At the very heart of Somerset is a large expanse of low-lying land, little of which rises more than 25 ft above sea level. This is the land of the Somerset Levels and Moors and includes wetlands of international importance to the world of conservation. Centuries ago, these low-lying areas were flooded for many months each year. Large elements still do flood from November right through to February, and the early morning view from the top of the Polden Hills is of clouds of rising mist lapping against the sides of the hills.

The Polden Hills, scattered with unique and picturesque villages, split the area, with peat moors to the north and clay moors to the south. It was the millennia of flooding, during which layer upon layer of alluvial silt was deposited, that created the clay so favoured by the potter and those who made bricks and tiles. John Leach, who lives down on the mist shrouded moors, is one such potter. He is the eldest grandson of the renowned potter Bernard Leach and is based at his thatched pottery in Muchelney, where an abbey, now in ruins, once stood. His designs can be found in museums and galleries across the world.

He has also created a wildlife reserve at his pottery, with a one-acre pond, which John describes as the best and most important thing he has ever made out of clay. It forms part of a conservation project that includes the planting of 4,000 broadleaf trees which, when mature, will provide the materials for craftsmen of the future. It is a most unusual and worthy example of one man at harmony with the landscape from which he takes his raw materials and to which he returns the favour many times over.

SEDGEMOOR, THE LAST BATTLE ON ENGLISH SOIL

And when old Sedgemoor's plain was gained,
The foe upon their track,
The fickle star of fortune waned
On Monmouth's rash attack.

E. H. BURRINGTON, *Monmouth*

Standing proud over King's Sedgemoor is an area of steep-sided high ground, along one side of which runs the ancient Aller Wood. Beneath the woods can be found two hamlets, Beer and Stout. Down on the Levels, at just a few feet above sea level, can be found some of the lushest grassland in the country, which makes the area particularly suitable for dairy farming. Thus, Friesian cattle are the most familiar of the grazing animals, with the exception perhaps of the shy but nonetheless common roe deer.

To maintain the moisture required during the dry summer months and to facilitate the drainage in winter, the Levels are criss-crossed by a network of ditches, rhynes and rivers, some natural but mostly man-made.

Just a few miles across the moors can be found the 'Zoy' villages of Westonzoyland, Middlezoy and Chedzoy. *Zoy* is thought to be an old Somerset word for island and reflects how these settlements were created on areas of ground which stood sufficiently high to keep them clear of the winter floods. It was in the midst of those villages that the Battle of Sedgemoor took place in July 1685, when the Duke of Monmouth took his rebel army from the town of Bridgwater out onto the moor under cover of darkness. The accidental firing of a musket gave the alarm to the camp where the king's troops were at rest. Before the night was over, hundreds of rebels had lost their lives and thousands were being hunted across the fields and hills of King's Sedgemoor and the Poldens.

THE PARRETT BASIN

Parrett, thou art Old Ocean's lawful daughter,
And to her breast thou rushest down with glee!

E. H. BURRINGTON, *Apostrophe to the Parrett*

For centuries the River Parrett served as the main artery for the movement of trade goods around Somerset. It is the one river which, through its tributaries, reaches from the sea deep into the county – to Bridgwater, Taunton, Langport and beyond. In the days of green roads, the river was the only way to transport goods into the Somerset hinterland, using sailing ships in the deeper reaches as far as Bridgwater and then barges.

It is the River Parrett into which the rainfall collects from the surrounding hills: the Mendips, Blackdowns, Brendons and Quantocks. But the Parrett basin is a flat landscape, much of which is below sea level. So flat is the landscape that a rise in the land level of just a few feet is sufficient for that area to be called an island, reflecting the days when most of this area was permanently below water.

It is a land which without man's interference would consist of swamp and marsh. And so, over the centuries a system of drainage has been introduced, consisting of rhynes (locally pronounced *reens*) and drains, the latter being huge man-made rivers. They all eventually

link into the tidal River Parrett. Where they link, there are strategically placed clyses, huge valve-like systems which allow water to flow out at low tide but stop the inward flow when the tide turns. The very word Sedgemoor (King's Sedgemoor, Queen's Sedgemoor and West Sedgemoor), tells its own story. And its system of walls to keep water out and drains to take it away was installed in medieval times. This allowed crops to be grown with greater confidence of a successful harvest.

The natural wetness of the area makes it ideal for growing withies, young stems of willow, from which the local wicker products are made. Basket and chair making using withies requires strong hands and arms. The weaver's tools are few: a bodkin, a sharp knife, secateurs and a beating iron, which is used to knock the withies into place. Traditionally, baskets are made with the craftsman sitting on the floor, his back against the wall and a board on his lap to keep the finished product level. It is back breaking, hard work which takes years to learn, just like the growing of the willows themselves in the acres of withy beds.

WHERE THE CIDER APPLES GROW

Their orchards might well be styled their temples,
And Apple Trees their Idols of Worship ...

WILLIAM MARSHALL, 1796

Cider and Somerset are synonymous. It was not that many years ago that every farm would have at least one cider orchard, since cider formed part of the worker's wages. An agricultural labourer would perhaps be paid seven shillings a week, plus a shilling's worth of cider. It formed an essential part of the social fabric of Somerset rural life. Across the county apple orchards could be found with varieties such as Morgan Sweet and Kingston Black. Sadly many of those orchards have gone. It was a system of grants which encouraged the destruction of the orchards and it is a system of grants which now encourages their regeneration.

November is harvest time for cider apples, which are collected from the orchard floor after they have fallen. The trees are often shaken or the branches beaten to hasten the process. Once gathered in, the apples are crushed in a mill before they are finally pressed to extract the juice. To make pure and true cider, nothing else is added or taken away. The apples come with a natural yeast on the skins, which is all that is needed to start the fermentation process.

Prior to Roman times, the Celts and their predecessors valued apple trees, not for their fruit, which was a sharp inedible crab apple, but for the mistletoe which grew on them and was important in various pagan rites. It was the Romans who originally introduced edible apples and orchards to Britain and it was the Normans who introduced the art of cider making. By the end of the 13th century, cider formed an essential part of the rural economy and remained so until the early part of the 20th century. Partly through a poor image, cider fell from popularity over recent decades but now appears to be making a comeback, as indeed are Somerset's orchards.

ANCIENT ILMINSTER

A workman at Jordans, Ilminster, in 1796, who, with a prisoner at Taunton in 1714, used the blasphemous appeal "God strike me dead", and so were struck.

RUTH TONGUE, *Somerset Folklore*

It was here on the River Yeo, once known as the River Isle, that a minster church was built in the 7th century. The present minster church of St Mary's, cruciform in shape, and Perpendicular in style, can be found in Silver Street. It dates back to around 1500 and has an impressive 90 ft tower, apparently fashioned on that of Wells Cathedral. Within its walls are the tombs of Nicolas and Dorothy Wadham, who were co-founders of Wadham College in Oxford.

The town grew around the market square and much was destroyed by fire in 1491 and again in 1661. It was about that time that Ilminster was the fourth largest town in Somerset, its economy based firmly on cloth making, an industry which survived well into the 19th century. The market square has as its centrepiece a particularly attractive open-sided market house, supported by pillars. It was built in 1813 and appears to have replaced a timber built shambles from earlier times. Other notable buildings are the George Hotel with its 18th-century façade, noted now for Queen Victoria once having slept there and the 17th-century Bell Inn with its mullioned windows.

Just to the north of the town is Dillington House, set in its own parklands. There has been a house on the site for at least a thousand years; the present building dates back to the 16th century and was considerably rebuilt in the 1830s in the Jacobean style. It was originally the home of the Speke family, in whose possession it remained for 200 years; later it became the property of the Camerons and it has passed down through that family ever since. After a period when it remained empty, it was used in the war years by the Forces and thereafter was leased to Somerset County Council, which now uses it as a residential centre for adult education and for promoting the arts.

TO THE MANOR BORN

Shik-shaks gone and past
Thee's the biggest fool at last
When Shik-shak comes again
Thee'st be biggest fool then.

RUTH TONGUE, CREWKERNE APRIL FOOL SUPERSTITION, *Somerset Folklore*

Crewkerne, now with a population of some 8,000 people, can be traced back to Saxon times, when it had a royal mint as one of its industries. Coins bearing the name Crucern have been discovered in Scandinavia. The surrounding villages also reveal much of the history of the area: Hinton St George has medieval origins; Lopen lays claim to a magnificent Roman mosaic pavement; and there are many other villages which add to the beauty and character of the landscape around Crewkerne.

Crewkerne's economic fortunes were once based on textiles, in particular sail making. Nelson's *Victory* entered the Battle of Trafalgar with sails made in the town. And that wasn't the *Victory*'s only link with the town for the Flag Officer, Sir Thomas Hardy, was educated at Crewkerne Grammar School. Crewkerne's charm is enhanced by its many Georgian buildings. It is a town at the centre of a predominantly agricultural community. To the west of the market place is the mainly Perpendicular church of St Bartholomew, built of Ham stone on the site of an earlier Saxon church (*opposite*).

Close, along the road to Chard, can be found the village of Cricket St Thomas in a sheltered valley beneath the ridge of Windwhistle Hill (*inset*). Already famous for its wildlife park, it further came to prominence during the screening of the popular TV series *To the Manor Born*, which featured both the manor house and the gatehouse lodge. The house was once the home of Alexander Hood, who became Lord Bridport. He was the son of the vicar of Butleigh and became a naval commander. In similar fashion, his brother was to become an admiral and eventually Viscount Hood. On the death of Lord Bridport, who was childless, the estate passed to his great nephew, Samuel Hood, who married Nelson's niece Charlotte. It was he who created the landscaped features we can see today, damming the river to create a series of lakes. Family debts forced the sale of the house and it passed through a series of owners; today it belongs to a holiday company and serves as a hotel.

In Trust to the Nation – Montacute and Muchelney

Over-looking the moss-grown wall of the rook-haunted, garlic floored spinney down by the old Montacute Mill, I well remember in our nursery walks seeing a notice-board with the words 'Beware of Man Traps' still clearly legible upon its weather-worn wood …

LLEWELLYN POWYS, *Somerset Essays* (1937)

South Somerset is wonderfully rich in National Trust properties, and Montacute, with its grand house and magnificent gardens (*opposite*) provides a complete contrast to the quaint and humble Priest House in Mulchelney (*inset*).

Montacute village can be found three miles west of Yeovil. It dates back to 680 and had a number of names until the Normans declared it *Mons Acutus* 'pointed hill'. On that hill a Norman Castle disappeared, to be replaced by an 18th-century folly. The main square of Montacute village has many houses which are 17th and 18th-century, built from the local stone. There are also two quite attractive old inns, the late 17th-century Phelips Arms and the King's Arms, an 18th-century coaching house.

But it is Montacute House, surely one of the finest homes in the country, which draws the visitors. Built around 1600, it is H-shaped and late Elizabethan in style. On its second floor is the longest gallery in the country, which now houses a collection of 16th and 17th-century portraits from the National Portrait Gallery. The premises are surrounded by splendid gardens, in keeping with such an exquisite

house. In 1931 it was purchased by Ernest Cook, the grandson of Thomas Cook, the traveller.

Across the moors can be found Muchelney, together with the ruins of its 10th-century Benedictine abbey and the 12th-century thatched Priest House, which is surely one of the National Trust's smallest properties. As a religious centre, only Glastonbury can claim to have a longer history than Mulcheney. The clergy's appetite for fish is reflected in the Domesday Book entry for Muchelney, which shows not only a vineyard but two fisheries, from which were taken 6,000 eels each year.

Muchelney, which means 'large island', once again reflecting the low lying nature of much of Somerset, was built on the higher ground and on that also stands the 15th-century church, with its wagon roof and Norman tiles. It is in Mulcheney that John Leach the potter practises his craft in his thatched workshop. In 1990, during the February peak of the annual flooding, his was the last house on dry land, and the villagers had to row to it to pick up their supplies.

ANCIENT AND MODERN YEOVIL

Two of us in the churchyard lie,
My sister and my brother
And in the churchyard cottage, I
Dwell near them with my mother.

WILLIAM WORDSWORTH, *We are Seven*

Yeovil, overlooked by Wyndham Hill, is one of Somerset's largest towns and is certainly its 'border town'. Its economy is as dependent on the population of north Dorset as on that of South Somerset. Its origins certainly go back to Roman times, villas having been found at Lufton and High Ham and on the site of the local helicopter factory. Yeovil was a small town prior to the 19th century, with just a few thousand inhabitants.

Cloth making, glove making and tanning were the significant industries here, but these are now all but gone. Today, the town's principal industry is that of aerospace, with Westland Helicopters and Normalair, plus other associated enterprises.

The theme is further reflected at nearby Yeovilton, where the Fleet Air Arm has its base, together with an excellent museum. From here one can watch Harrier jump-jets going through their paces, and an increase in activity is usually a hint of some far-flung conflict needing an escalation of training.

South Somerset has many beautiful villages that benefit from the honey coloured local stone which gives a pleasant warm feel to many a country cottage. The rather grandly named Kingsbury Episcopi, with its lock-up on the village green, is one such example. The parish actually encompasses a number of small hamlets, such as Stembridge, Burrow, and Thorney (where the lowland games that take place annually include such wonderful country sports as welly throwing and mud wrestling). The parish also includes West, Mid and East Lambrook. The last of these, East Lambrook, has the 15th-century East Lambrook Manor – although it was never a manor. It was acquired by Margery and Walter Fish in 1937 and within its grounds they created a series of cottage style gardens (*inset*), which became highly popular through Margery's publication of a series of eight books.

BLEAK AND BEAUTIFUL MENDIP

Up the rude romantic glen, up the cliff and thro' the glade

SAMUEL TAYLOR COLERIDGE, TO THE REVEREND W. J. HORT ...

A land of many facets – stark and bleak, bare and wide open vistas creating a feeling of space, where the sky dominates the scene and long walls of mortarless grey stone bound the rolling fields – Mendip holds a secret, with deep, meandering caverns below ground, on a scale which suggests there is as much of Mendip to explore below the surface as there is above. The hills stretch for 20 miles from Brean Down in the west to Frome in the east, with their highest point at 1,068 ft at Black Down. Iron Age hill forts and ancient burial mounds such as those at Priddy Nine Barrows tell of a long history. Here the Romans mined lead, an industry which lasted right through to Victorian times, and the remains of their smelting works are still to be found at Charterhouse.

The Mendips have a wild and rugged beauty of their own, with huge craggy gorges, the grandest being Cheddar Gorge. Equal not in size but in beauty is Ebbor Gorge (*inset*), a dramatic cleft in the limestone rock. A path leads down through the woods here to limestone cliffs potted with caves where Stone Age man left clues to his habitation. Likewise in Cheddar Gorge, cave contents indicate the presence of Stone Age man and his prey, including hyenas and bears. In more recent times, the hills were part of the royal forests, and at Axbridge, on the lower slopes of the Mendips, is a house known as King John's Hunting Lodge.

This is excellent walking country, wild, open, and in many places barren. Those who are more adventurous can try the many underground caves and potholes, but local advice is recommended, especially if heavy rains are a possibility, as underground rivers can rapidly swell to fill the chambers. For lovers of wildlife, the landscape supports many rare examples of flora, some almost unique to the area as well as peregrine falcons, badgers, foxes and adders.

SPIRITUAL GLASTONBURY – LAND OF MYTHS AND LEGENDS

And did those feet in ancient times
walk upon England's mountains green?

WILLIAM BLAKE, *Jerusalem*

There is a uniqueness to Glastonbury which sets it apart from all other Somerset towns. Glastonbury is a centre of mysticism, myths and legends, a town which draws to its centre those of an alternative inclination: hippies, travellers, druids and those in search of religious experiences. The unmistakable Glastonbury Tor acts as a magnet to pilgrims of all persuasions, whether Christian, Druid or New Age,

and those simply drawn by the legend of King Arthur. It is said that here Arthur had his Round Table and in Glastonbury Abbey are the graves of Arthur and his Queen, Guinevere.

Glastonbury was the site of the earliest foundations of English Christianity on our shores. Ancient stories tell how Joseph of Arimathea sailed to Glastonbury on a mission to preach the gospel. He is believed to have brought the Holy Grail with him and buried it beneath Glastonbury's Tor, at the Chalice Well. At Wearyall Hill, on his route to Glastonbury, he stuck his staff in the ground and from it grew a thorn bush. The thorn blossoms in mid winter, and, as if to prove the legend, a flowering sprig is sent each Christmas to the Queen.

The tor itself is the very symbol of Glastonbury, and on its peak stands the ruin of St Michael's church. Here in AD 1000 there was an earthquake, leaving only the tower of the church still standing. In the town centre can be found the ruins of Glastonbury Abbey (*inset*), once one of the most powerful abbeys in the country and the very centre of ecclesiastical history in Somerset. Later it was at the heart of the revival of the monastic movement in western Europe. It played a pivotal role in the conversion from Celtic to Latin Christianity in Britain.

The nearby ancient abbey barn houses a wonderful Rural Life Museum, which contains a local willow with a split trunk, suggestive of a hernia and believed to be a cure for the same. Young children suffering from ruptures would be passed through the split and, so it was believed, the rupture would be cured.

The Charm of Cheddar

A wilder place for some romantic story,
Ne'er graced this rare and brave old land of ours,
A grander spot ne'er showed the living glory,
Of tree, and shrubs, and flowers.

E. H. Burrington, *Cheddar Cliffs*

The Grand Canyon of the West Country, Cheddar Gorge was carved out of the limestone rocks to present 500 ft high, neck craning, sheer cliffs. It was worn away by the river thousands of years ago. The river has now been replaced by a road and only at times of high rainfall does it give warning as to how it once rushed down in torrents as it re-visits the cleft it created. The cliff faces are home to rare plant life, such as Cheddar pinks and alpine pennycress. From the lower end of the gorge, where the ancient town of Cheddar stands, the 274 steps of Jacob's Ladder provide a safe ascent to the top of the gorge, heart and lungs permitting.

At the base of the gorge are a number of caves. It was in 1837 that George Cox discovered them and realised their potential for visitors. In 1903 skeletons dating back over 10,000 years were revealed and these are now in the local museum. In 1890 Richard Cox discovered further caves, which went half a mile deep under the Mendip Hills through chambers carved by the River Yeo. Amongst the innermost chambers are some of the larger ones discovered in 1898, the year the caves were opened to the public.

Cheddar is, of course, famous for its cheese. Sadly for the local population, the name Cheddar is considered generic. But here in the town, the visitor can witness real Cheddar cheese being made, using the milk from the large herds of Friesian cattle so common in this dairy dominated part of Somerset. Almost as famous as its cheese, Cheddar strawberries are the main summer crop and field after field of strawberry beds can be seen along the road from Cheddar to Axbridge and Draycott.

COMPTON MARTIN AND AXBRIDGE

Having quitted Cheddar in a heavy storm of rain, and driven through Axbridge Cross,
I fell in with a troop of gypsies who had a train of donkeys carrying their baggage before them.

REV. JOHN SKINNER, *Journal of a Somerset Rector*

Nestling beneath the northern escarpment of the Mendip Hills lie the scenic Chew Valley and Blagdon lakes. Compton Martin lies on the main road between these two large reservoirs at the head of the valleys of the River Chew and Congresbury Yeo. It is a picturesque village with its post office and whitewashed cottages overlooking the village pond.

The village must be one of Somerset's earliest settlements, with evidence provided by the discovery in a pit of Beaker pottery from the Neolithic period, over 4,000 years ago, and nearby can be found tumuli and pre-historic hut circles.

At one time teasels were grown and harvested here to supply the cloth trade in Bristol and Wiltshire, and some were exported to Yorkshire, shipped via the River Yeo and the network of inland waterways. Around 1800 the whole teasel industry, which thrived in Compton Martin and neighbouring Ubley and East and West Harptree, suddenly and inexplicably moved to the valley of the River Isle in South Somerset and has remained there every since.

Compton Martin has one of the finest Norman churches in the county, St Michael's, with its unusually large porch, vaulted chancel, a 16th-century tower, and pillars dating back to 1150. But today it is perhaps the lakes which are the main attraction. The magnificent 1,200 acre Chew Valley Lake, opened in 1952 to serve the needs of nearby Bristol, can claim to have the best trout lake fishing in Europe and is an important wintering site for tens of thousands of wildfowl with its large reed beds. The nearby Blagdon Lake, which opened in 1902, is smaller and somewhat overshadowed by its neighbour but is the more picturesque of the two. Both are well worth a visit.

Axbridge lies beneath the southern edge of the Mendips. It was once a medieval hunting centre and many buildings still exist from that period. In the town square, where bull baiting and cock fighting once took place, can be found King John's Hunting Lodge (*inset*), which was probably a merchant's house and is now a museum; a 15th-century almshouse now serves as a restaurant. The town hall and Lamb Hotel both belong to the early 19th century, whilst the Old Angel Inn dates back to 1550.

THE WICKED WITCH OF WOOKEY

In aunciente days, tradition showes,
A base and wicked elfe arose
The Witch of Wokey hight.

DR HENRY HARRINGTON, *The Witch of Wokey*

Beneath the Mendip Hills lie 15 miles of explored caves and an estimated 200 miles yet to be discovered. Amongst the most magnificent of all those caves are the ones at Wookey Hole, which have yielded the remains of rhinoceros, reindeer, wolf and early man. There is even a hyena's den, containing the teeth from over 450 hyenas – along with those of other early inhabitants.

Access to the caves, through which flows the River Axe, is generally for specialist cave divers only, but a large and spectacular part is open throughout the year to the public. Huge stalactites and stalagmites form fascinating patterns as one enters the chambers, the second of which stands at 75 ft high. The third chamber is the Witch's Parlour and here can be seen the petrified form of the Witch of Wookey. According to legend, this once beautiful witch was sprinkled with holy water by a young monk and with that she was turned to stone. It seems to be no way for a young monk to treat a lady, but, if the story is true, she was at the time cooking a young child she had stolen from the village!

In the public area, the river flows into an idyllically blue lake, which provides a deceptive picture of complete stillness whilst hiding the movement of the millions of gallons of water flowing by. So clean and pure is the water that it lends itself to paper making, a small industry, which has a considerable history at Wookey dating back to 1610. Today small quantities of high quality paper are produced at the Victorian mill using the old fashioned hand-made methods. The quality of Wookey paper was such that it was used for bank notes and Queen Victoria's writing paper. Visitors to the caves can even have a go at making their own.

Also to be seen are the rows and rows of 'has-beens' from Madame Tussaud's Waxworks. As new exhibits are added to the London collection, so those who are perhaps of less interest are taken away and sent to Wookey, where the constant underground climatic conditions are perfect for the long-term protection of the numerous disconnected heads.

MAJESTY AND SPLENDOUR AT WELLS

At Wells ... I preached on the shady side of the market-place ...

JOHN WESLEY, *Journal* 29 August 1780

There can be no doubting the majesty and splendour of Wells Cathedral, especially when viewed on a summer's evening, as the setting sunlight illuminates the west face with a softened honey coloured glow. It was on such an evening I took two American visitors to view this monument, the earliest and best surviving example of English Gothic architecture, with its 365 statues, perhaps the finest collection in Europe. As we passed from the town square, through Penniless Porch, the scene opened before us, leaving my visitors with jaws dropped in wonderment. Never in their world travels had they witnessed such fine medieval architecture.

Christianity on this site dates back to Roman times. Recent excavations revealed a Roman mausoleum and Saxon chapels. Cathedral status was granted in 909 and construction of the new cathedral began in 1180, the towers to the left and right having been added some 200 years later. It was Adam Lock, a local mason, who takes much of the credit for its design, and his bust adorns the cathedral walls as a lasting testament to his endeavours. Inside the cathedral, the octagonal chapter house with its splendid fan-vaulted ceiling is reached by a set of steps which have the appearance of sea-worn rocks. Beyond the chapter house, where cathedral affairs are still determined by members of the chapter, the stairs extend to cross over the road to Vicar's Close (*inset*), Europe's oldest medieval street, proudly still intact. This group of 42 houses was built to house the vicars choral, the canon's deputies at cathedral services. To the south of the cathedral lies the moated bishop's palace with its famous swan bell.

In the town square, brass plaques in the pavement record the distance achieved when local girl Mary Bignall Rand broke the Olympic long jump record.

CRUMBLING CASTLES

There be diverse praty towrres in the utter Warde of the Castelle

JOHN LELAND, 1540

Close to the county border with Wiltshire stand the extensive remains of Farleigh Hungerford Castle (*opposite*), built in the 1370s by Sir Thomas Hungerford, the first Speaker of the House of Commons. He rather cheekily built it without royal licence but was pardoned later for his presumption. It is defended to the north and east by a natural dyke and on the other two sides by a ditch. It was built to be impressive, as a demonstration of strength and power, and it was built to look old. It was important to the Hungerfords to create the impression of being established rather than nouveau rich.

Today, the castle is largely in ruins but a feeling of its past importance is easily gained and its commanding position overlooking the river can be appreciated. On Sir Thomas's death, his son Walter took over. He distinguished himself as a soldier and also became the Speaker of the House of Commons. He contributed to the castle by adding its outer court and in so doing he enclosed the parish church within the precincts of the castle. With that the village of Farleigh became Farleigh Hungerford.

Nearby Nunney Castle (*inset*) was built around the same time, 1373. Sir John Delamere, however, was granted a royal licence to crenellate from Edward III. At Nunney the church already occupied the most commanding position, and so Sir John built the castle on a low lying spot. Tall and rectangular, it has round towers at each corner. But it lacked the impressive strength of Farleigh Hungerford. Nunney's castle has relatively thin walls, incapable of withstanding an artillery attack. It failed miserably in the Civil War when guns were placed on the surrounding higher ground – the walls were breached almost with the first cannon fire. It was a small castle and though it can boast possibly the deepest moat in England, it lacked even a portcullis. But it has a quaint charm and is well worth a visit.

CAMELOT COUNTRY

Yesterday something wonderful. It was a golden day and the apple blossoms are out and for the first time I climbed up to Cadbury – Camelot. I don't think I remember such an impact like that.

JOHN STEINBECK, describing his stay in Somerset, 1st May 1959

This is the land of Arthurian legend. The charming village of South Cadbury is dominated by the nearby hill-fort site of Cadbury Castle, the Camelot of Arthurian legend. This wooded hill served as a fort as far back as the Iron Age and is one of the best examples in southern Britain. It began life as a Neolithic settlement around 300 BC. Then it grew from its modest Bronze Age beginnings to a spectacular Iron Age site, with as many as three religious temples from the period around 500 BC.

For a while the Romans had a military presence here after they attacked the fort around AD 60 and the inhabitants were massacred or if lucky just driven away. It was rebuilt as a fort around AD 470 to protect against the invading Saxons and was built on a major scale such as would require a huge army of labour. Large stone walls encircled the camp, with wooden walkways on which the native warriors patrolled. Pottery from the time of Arthur and other finds suggest this was the site of a great chieftain, a site of significant social and military status. It all ties in with the theory that this was Arthur's Camelot.

Nearby can be found the quaint village of Queen Camel (*inset*), the queen being Eleanor, who owned it in the 13th century. Camel is possibly a Celtic name derived from *canto* meaning border and *mel*, a bore hill. The stone houses here are built with the local blue lias, and many of them are thatched. Maintaining that feeling of yesteryear, a cobbled lane leads to the church of St Barnabus, whose tower – which unusually for this part of the country is in five stages – is claimed to contain the heaviest peal of six bells in the world.

Images of Old England

The free, fair Homes of England!
Long, long, in hut and hall,
May hearts of native proof be rear'd
To guard each hallow'd wall!

Felicia Hemans, *The Homes of England*

Straddling the River Brue, Bruton is a town whose pattern of compact streets and alleyways reflects its medieval origins. Its buildings of Doulting stone create a town full of character and much in harmony. Amongst these splendid buildings are the 15th-century Abbey Court House and Hugh Sexey's Hospital, a fine Jacobean almshouse from 1638. Both can be found in the main street. The town is probably of late Saxon origin, and at the time of Canute coins were struck here in his name. An Augustine priory was founded in 1130 and gained abbey status in 1511, but little evidence remains today, except for the 16th-century dovecote (*opposite*) and a high stone perimeter wall along Plox Street.

The church of St Mary is one of the best in the area, with its magnificent Perpendicular west tower, built in 1480 and standing at over 100 ft. Other parts of the church date back to the 14th and 15th centuries and testify to the prosperity of Bruton from its woollen cloth trade. This lasted until the end of the 18th century, when, owing to the diminishing demand it was replaced in part by silk spinning and weaving.

At Lytes Cary (*inset*) we can find the charming medieval manor house where Henry Lyte, the herbalist, once lived and created a botanical garden. Such was his expertise that *Lyte's Herbal* when published in 1578 became a best seller and was still being reprinted as late as 1678. Wandering around the gardens, high hedges of yew topiary conceal aspects of the garden design which are suddenly revealed to the visitor. Fountains and statues offer formality, and yet there is a simplicity which is in balance with the stone-built house.

In 1775, after around 500 years in the ownership of the Lyte family, the property was sold to the Dickinsons. In 1907, to the benefit of the nation, Sir Walter Jenner set about its rescue from the state into which it had fallen, restoring not just the house and gardens, but replacing the interior furnishings as well. He bequeathed the property to the National Trust and it remains today in their safe custody.

FROME – CHAPELS AND CHURCHES

The town hath a good meetly market and is set on the cliff of a stony hill.

JOHN LELAND, 1545

The establishment of Frome, one of Somerset's smaller towns, dates back to 688, when a church was founded by St Aldhelm. This is a hilly town, where steep roads run down the hillsides to the River Frome, on which the town stands. From its medieval days it was noted for its cloth making and once supplied seven wagon loads of cloth each week to London. It was an industry which was to survive until fairly recent times, outlasting that in many other towns in this part of Somerset. For centuries, the town and its surrounding villages depended on the one industry, but the 19th century brought its decline and with that the growth of the previously expanding town stabilised.

Frome's expansion then restarted in the 1960s, as it increasingly became a commuter town for Bristol, Bath and even Swindon, and since then it has doubled in size. It has, however, maintained the majority of its historic buildings and street patterns and can boast more listed buildings, mostly Grade II, than any other Mendip town. One such building is Rook Lane chapel, the site of which was gifted on his death by the family of Robert Smith. It was built in 1707 and is arguably the finest Congregational chapel in the region.

But older and finer still is St John's church, which dates back to the 15th century with its beautiful tower and spire. It was possibly built on the site where St Aldhelm had his settlement. If so, it is equally probable that it was the freshwater spring which brought him here. The same stream runs down through the centre of Cheap Street in the heart of the town. This street is a pedestrian passage, lined with some of the oldest shops in Frome, which lean inwards from each side. Catherine Hill, once a key shopping street, is a steep and narrow cobbled road, which maintains its charm, although it has lost its sparkle as the centre for shopping has shifted elsewhere. This is a town worth exploring since much of its character lies behind the immediate façade of its through roads.